HAL•LEONARD
INSTRUMENTAL
PLAY-ALONG

AUDIO
ACCESS
INCLUDED

PLAYBACK+
Speed • Pitch • Balance • Loop

CLARINET

Disney Greats

T0055339

ISBN 978-0-634-08540-6

Walt Disney Music Company
Wonderland Music Company, Inc.

DISTRIBUTED BY

HAL•LEONARD®
CORPORATION
7777 W. BLUEMOUND RD. P.O. BOX 13819 MILWAUKEE, WI 53213

Visit Hal Leonard Online at
www.halleonard.com

Title	Page

ARABIAN NIGHTS
from Walt Disney's ALADDIN

Clarinet

Lyrics by HOWARD ASHMAN
Music by ALAN MENKEN

THE BARE NECESSITIES

from Walt Disney's THE JUNGLE BOOK

Clarinet

Words and Music by
TERRY GILKYSON

A CHANGE IN ME

from Walt Disney's BEAUTY AND THE BEAST: THE BROADWAY MUSICAL

CLARINET

Words by TIM RICE
Music by ALAN MENKEN

HAWAIIAN ROLLER COASTER RIDE

from Walt Disney's LILO & STITCH

CLARINET

Words and Music by ALAN SILVESTRI
and MARK KEALI'I HO'OMALU

HONOR TO US ALL

from Walt Disney Pictures' MULAN

CLARINET

Music by MATTHEW WILDER
Lyrics by DAVID ZIPPEL

◆ I'M STILL HERE

(Jim's Theme)

from Walt Disney's TREASURE PLANET

CLARINET

Words and Music by
JOHN RZEZNIK

IT'S A SMALL WORLD

from "IT'S A SMALL WORLD" at Disneyland Park and Magic Kingdom Park

CLARINET

Words and Music by RICHARD M. SHERMAN
and ROBERT B. SHERMAN

THE MEDALLION CALLS

from Walt Disney Pictures' PIRATES OF THE CARIBBEAN: THE CURSE OF THE BLACK PEARL

CLARINET

Music by KLAUS BADELT

LOOK THROUGH MY EYES

from Walt Disney Pictures' BROTHER BEAR

CLARINET

Words and Music by
PHIL COLLINS

15

PROMISE

from MILLENNIUM CELEBRATION at Epcot

CLARINET

Music by GAVIN GREENAWAY
Words by DON DORSEY

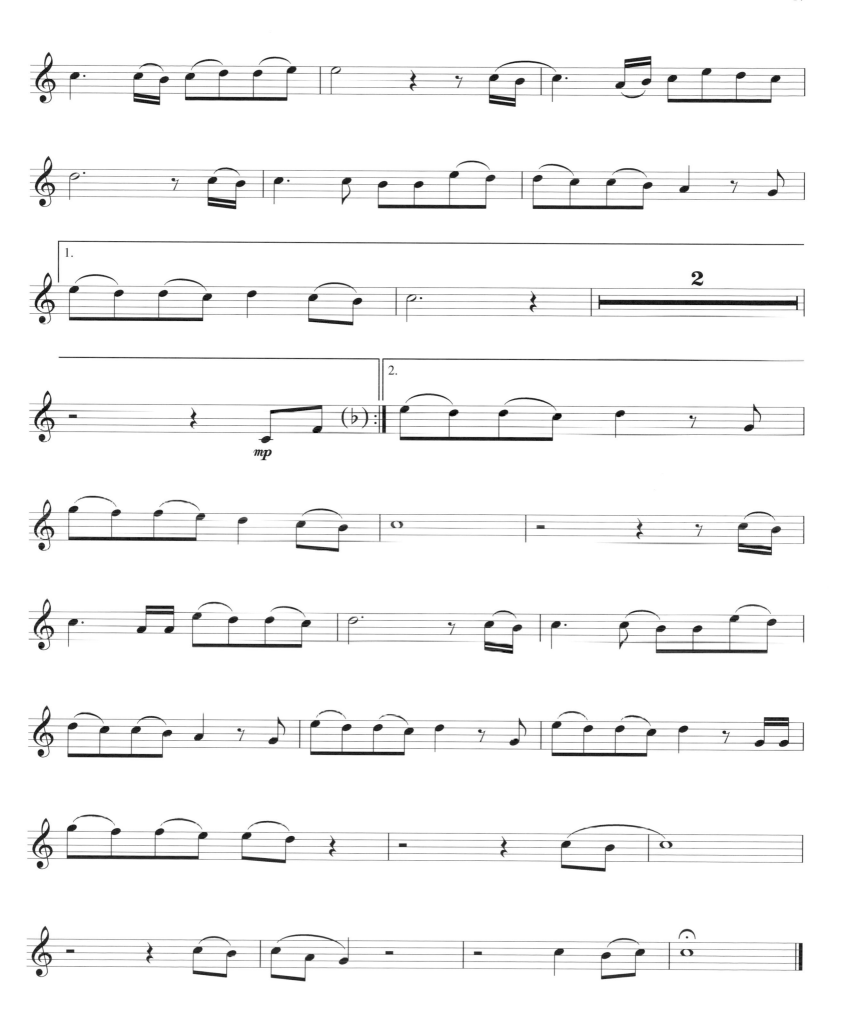

THE SIAMESE CAT SONG

from Walt Disney's LADY AND THE TRAMP

CLARINET

Words and Music by PEGGY LEE
and SONNY BURKE

SUPERCALIFRAGILISTICEXPIALIDOCIOUS

from Walt Disney's MARY POPPINS

Clarinet

Words and Music by RICHARD M. SHERMAN
and ROBERT B. SHERMAN

TWO WORLDS

from Walt Disney Pictures' TARZAN™

CLARINET

Words and Music by
PHIL COLLINS

WHERE THE DREAM TAKES YOU

from Walt Disney Pictures' ATLANTIS: THE LOST EMPIRE

CLARINET

Lyrics by DIANE WARREN
Music by DIANE WARREN and JAMES NEWTON HOWARD

YO HO
(A Pirate's Life for Me)
from PIRATES OF THE CARIBBEAN at Disneyland Park and Magic Kingdom Park

CLARINET

Words by XAVIER ATENCIO
Music by GEORGE BRUNS